South Amesbury's Red Earthenware & Stoneware

The 1791-1820 William Pecker Pottery

Justin W. Thomas

Historic Beverly

Beverly Massachusetts

Copyright © 2021 by **Justin W. Thomas**

All rights reserved. No part of this publication may be reproduced, distributed or transmitted in any form or by any means, without prior written permission.

Justin W. Thomas/Historic Beverly
117 Cabot Street
Beverly MA 01915
Historicbeverly.net

South Amesbury's Red Earthenware & Stoneware: The 1791-1820 William Pecker Pottery/ Justin W. Thomas. -- 1st ed.

ISBN 978-1-891906-22-0

Dedicated to my niece, Alexis, nephew, Jason, my parents and my sister, Meghan.

"Our greatest weakness lies in giving up. The most certain way to succeed is always to try just one more time."

–THOMAS EDISON

> Contents

Preface | 7

Introduction | 15

1. South Amesbury's Eighteenth Century Production and the Potters Who Followed | 29
2. The Site of the William Pecker Pottery | 51
3. South Amesbury's Red Earthenware and Archaeology | 58
4. South Amesbury's Stoneware and Archaeology | 69
5. William Pecker's Exports and Museum Collections | 91
6. William Pecker's Legacy | 98
7. Illustrations | 103
    a. Partially Glazed Household Wares | 104
    b. Glazed Household Wares | 108
    c. Stoneware | 176

Appendix:
Bibliography | 194

> Preface

In the late 1990s, my father brought home an eighteenth or early nineteenth century black glazed red earthenware jug from a local flea market in Rowley, Massachusetts. I have since learned this jug was most likely made at one of the potteries located in South Danvers (known as Peabody after 1855), Essex County, Massachusetts.

For years, that jug sat in my parent's dining room, and ever now-and-again, I would pick it up out of curiosity, wondering about its history. I guess you can say that jug is what led to a nearly twenty year search, collecting eighteenth and nineteenth century red earthenware from all over America, although my focus has always remained with the early pottery made in New England.

As the years passed, I really wanted to learn the history about that black glazed jug: who made it, where it was made and what was it used for around the household. I often handled it, eventually setting out on my own to find some examples, even though I really had no idea about the aesthetics and rarity of some red earthenware that I am so drawn to today.

I found some pieces here-and-there, but it was at an Americana auction at Skinner in Boston in the fall of 2006 that changed my entire perspective about the appeal of red earthenware.

By this time, I had already been studying Massachusetts author Lura Woodside Watkins' (1897-1982) landmark book, *Early New England Potters and Their Wares*; the book gave me an incredible introduction to pottery made all over New England, but especially the Essex County wares manufactured local to where I grew up in Newburyport, Massachusetts. I learned about a potter named William Pecker (1758-1820), who worked only a few miles from my house in the village of South Amesbury (known as Merrimacport after 1876), Massachusetts. He was supposedly this prolific red earthenware potter; illustrated in Watkins' book in figures 40, 41 and 58 are examples of Merrimacport production that I would often reference, but these photos were published in black and white. I had never actually seen or held an example of red earthenware from the Pecker Pottery. These pieces are owned today by the National Museum of American History at the Smithsonian Institute in Washington, D.C. and Old Sturbridge Village in Sturbridge, Massachusetts; I have since visited these museums a number of times to study their pottery collections, but back in 2006, I had never actually held a piece of Pecker Pottery or seen any of the company's glazes in color.

I vividly remember going to that auction at Skinner on November 4, 2006; it was a special Saturday afternoon sale, where the Americana Collection of Denny L. & Patty Tracey was sold. I was basically just a spectator, buying three pieces of red earthenware that I still own today – one was made on Prince Edward Island in Canada in the late 1800s, another was made in Pennsylvania about 1850, and the third, a small nineteenth century jug from Maine. But I really had my eyes set on a nearly mint condition red earthenware jug (picture 21) made at the Pecker Pottery that was the color of a pumpkin and brushed with a black colored decoration (manganese). I can still recall holding that jug for the first time during the auction preview; it was so round, you could feel the skill of the potter by how refined the jug was. Alas, though, it sold for a lot more money than I could afford at the time.

Red earthenware purchased at Skinner in 2006; left to right: Prince Edward Island Jar, Maine jug and a Pennsylvania jar.

Eighteenth or early nineteenth century red earthenware jug attributed to South Danvers (Peabody), Mass. that my father Richard Thomas brought home from an Essex County, Massachusetts flea market in the 1990s. This jug is what helped ignite my interest in early American pottery; ht. 7 ½".

However, seeing this collection really changed my entire perspective on how a collection could be assembled, thinking to myself, "*I hope I can own a collection of pottery like this someday.*"

Even with this experience and some knowledge, though, I found it very difficult to find any pottery made at the William Pecker Pottery. At the time, it was clearly very collectible, where it is still just as much desired today. It is also rare; most of the pottery made in Merrimacport was discarded years ago, but a handful of pieces do survive.

I also learned about a mysterious stoneware jar decorated with a stamped bird and flower that was found at a Kentucky flea market, published in the 2004 edition of *Ceramics in America;* the jar was stamped "*Wm Pecker.*" There were so many questions that surrounded this jar because William Pecker was not considered to be a stoneware potter. The jar was slightly deformed, having been slumped on one side from an accident that happened in the kiln, although undoubtedly still a very important piece of pottery. To my knowledge, at the time, I thought it was a one of a kind piece of stoneware, where some very well respected longtime dealers in New England said that they had never seen a piece before.

William Pecker Pottery red earthenware pot that sold in the Olmstead Collection and later in Lew Scranton's Collection at Skinner in 2016 (courtesy Skinner Inc.).

As my search continued, I thought I had a better chance at purchasing my first piece of Pecker Pottery when the Dan and Jan Olmstead Collection sold in Portsmouth, New Hampshire on September 13, 2008. I went to the auction with my mother, who helped me keep track of what each lot of red earthenware sold for; I had my eyes set on lot number ten, a beautifully decorated red earthenware pot made at the Pecker Pottery. Once again, though, it was out of my price range, selling for nearly $9,000 (including the buyer's premium) to Killingworth, Connecticut antiques collector and dealer, Lewis Scranton (1936-2019). Lew had one of the great all-time collections of New England red earthenware, and he kept this piece in his personal collection until 2016, when he sold his collection through Skinner at a memorable onsite sale held at his house.

The Olmsteads owned other pieces of red earthenware made at the Pecker Pottery that I eventually acquired from Lew in 2010. I remember I was so excited when I finally bought that first piece; it took nearly five years, and I was thrilled with it. I have since assembled a collection of about fifty pieces of pottery made in Merrimacport, which I believe is a large percentage of the pieces known to exist today.

This book not only examines the red earthenware made at the Pecker Pottery, but also the site of the red earthenware business that I discovered by chance with my nephew Jason. But our most important discovery happened almost ten years ago, while we were on a bike ride, finding the site where Pecker actually produced stoneware. It was a miraculous discovery that has led to so much more information, proving that for a time, Pecker simultaneously operated a stoneware business aside his red earthenware production in South Amesbury.

William Pecker Pottery red earthenware pot (courtesy John McInnis).

This book is the most extensive study ever published about Merrimacport pottery, focusing on William Pecker's circa 1791-1820 production, but also taking into account what was made in Merrimacport before William Pecker at the Benjamin Bodge Pottery, as well as by Pecker's relatives, the Chase family, who produced red earthenware through the 1880s.

Upon completing this book, I visited the site of the William Pecker Pottery in Merrimacport once last time with my niece Alexis, just in case something significant had appeared that should be noted. I was surprised when she said, *"Coming here brings back so many memories!"* And it really does seeing that my nephew and niece have grown up around making these discoveries with me in Merrimacport, much of which has been lost, somewhat forgotten and rediscovered through time. I hope you enjoy reading this book as much as I enjoyed putting it together through the years.

Justin W. Thomas
2021

My niece Alexis with a piece of red earthenware kiln furniture that we discovered partially submerged in mud in Merrimacport, Mass. in January 2021.

The William Pecker Pottery

My nephew Jason at the site of the Pecker Pottery after discovering a number of red earthenware artifacts in 2013.

My nephew Jason at the site of the Pecker Pottery after discovering a number of red earthenware artifacts in 2013.

My nephew Jason at the site of the Pecker Pottery after discovering a number of stoneware artifacts in 2014.

My nephew Jason at the site of the Pecker Pottery after discovering a number of stoneware artifacts in 2014.

The William Pecker Pottery

> Introduction

The red earthenware made in Essex County, Massachusetts is some of the earliest and more skilled wares manufactured anywhere in New England. The most identifiable red earthenware manufactured in Essex County today is probably the wares that were manufactured in South Danvers (Peabody), Massachusetts.

The potteries in Charlestown, Massachusetts were the center of the red earthenware industry in New England before the American Revolution. The industry was all, but destroyed when British soldiers attacked Charlestown at the Battle of Bunker Hill on June 17, 1775. A few potters rebuilt and produced red earthenware after the revolution into the late eighteenth and nineteenth century, although the industry's impact on New England was never the same.

America's newfound independence seemed to inspire red earthenware potters throughout coastal New England, which saw many new businesses emerge after 1780. This growth continued into the 1800s, which corresponded with the birth of new towns and cities throughout the region.

Overall, there are at least 100 documented potters, producing red earthenware in Peabody in the eighteenth and nineteenth centuries. However, that total does not entirely reflect undocumented potters, as well as traveling potters and apprentices. It is very difficult to be sure of every potter working at a business, especially if some of those potters were only employed for a short period.

The Osborns are probably the most well known of any of the businesses that operated in Peabody. A Quaker potter, Joseph Osborn (1702-1780) established the first Osborn Pottery in about 1736. It began as a small business, but it grew as the company passed through generations of Osborn family ownership.

The William Pecker Pottery

Besides the Osborns, there were plenty of other successful potteries in Peabody, such as the Cook Pottery, the Goldthwaite Pottery, the Kettle or Kettel Pottery, the Proctor Pottery, the Stone Pottery, the Trask Pottery, the Whittemore Pottery and the Wilson Pottery. The majority of these businesses were founded in the eighteenth century and shared the Quaker faith with the Osborns.

Records indicate that as many as thirty-four potters from the Peabody/Salem area were listed in the local military that marched to Lexington in April 1775 – and there were at least thirty potteries producing red earthenware in this area during the War of 1812.

Many different forms were produced in Peabody: jars, pots, crocks, pans, cups, mugs, pitchers, vases, yarn holders, jugs, cruets, spittoons, foot warmers, porringers, bowls and plates were all common products at one time.

Neighboring Salem was a hot spot for the Peabody potters to sell their wares, although Peabody pottery has been recovered in various contexts in Essex County and in the Boston area. Ultimately, the potteries in the Peabody area became the largest red earthenware industry in New England in the late eighteenth and nineteenth century.

Interestingly, a number of the forms manufactured in Peabody were similar in shape to some of the wares manufactured at the circa 1764-1799 Daniel Bayley Pottery in Newburyport, Massachusetts.

South Danvers (Peabody), Mass. red earthenware; glazes can be mistaken for wares made in South Amesbury (Merrimacport), Mass.

The William Pecker Pottery

South Danvers (Peabody), Mass. red earthenware; glazes can be mistaken for wares made in South Amesbury (Merrimacport), Mass.

South Danvers (Peabody), Mass. red earthenware; glazes can be mistaken for wares made in South Amesbury (Merrimacport), Mass.

The William Pecker Pottery

Possibly all South Danvers (Peabody), Mass. red earthenware; (left) pitcher found in southern Maine, but possibly from South Danvers; (middle) jar is similar in form to jars made in Bristol County, Mass., but the manufacture and weight of this piece is different; (right) pitcher attributed to the Moses Paige Pottery in Peabody.

Large coastal Massachusetts red earthenware jar, probably eighteenth century in origin.

Almost ninety years after Newbury, Massachusetts was settled, the first known local pottery was established about 1723 by Joseph Bayley (1701-1761), a direct descendent of James Bayley (1612-1677) who was among the first group of settlers in Rowley, Massachusetts in 1639. It has not been identified where Bayley was taught the pottery craft, but he may have learned about it from another Essex County potter or possibly in Charlestown.

Joseph and his wife left Rowley in 1735, when they were removed from the church, and relocated with their four children to Newbury (Newburyport). Joseph continued to produce red earthenware in Newbury until the early 1760s, when his son Daniel (1729-1792) became owner of the business. Daniel must have learned the pottery business from this father, but there is also evidence to suggest he operated a pottery in Gloucester, Massachusetts, in the 1750s, when he married Elizabeth Dennen (d. 1765) from Gloucester on April 21, 1750. The couple spent the next decade in Gloucester, where they had three children, but only two survived. Elizabeth Bayley was born April 2, 1753 and Daniel Bayley Jr. (1755-1799) was born July 15, 1755, eventually becoming a potter himself.

By 1763, Daniel had relocated to High Street next to St. Paul's Church in Newbury, which became Newburyport the following year. This is where he built the pottery business he is known for today. Sadly, his wife died two years later, and he quickly married a woman named Sarah Stone (d. 1792), a widow herself and mother to three children. Soon after, they had four more kids, two of whom also entered the pottery industry, William Bayley (1766-1799) born May 9, 1766 and Nathaniel Bayley (1771-1849) born June 16, 1771.

Slip decorated pan attributed to the Bayley Pottery in Newburyport recovered within a circa late 1760s or early 1770s archaeological context at the site of a trading post in Saint John, New Brunswick (courtesy New Brunswick Museum).

The William Pecker Pottery

The Bayley Pottery turned into a family enterprise for the next few decades, largely capitalizing on local demand, although Bayley Pottery has also been recovered from archaeological contexts in Salem, Portsmouth, New Hampshire and as far north as Colonial trading posts in Veazie, Maine and Saint John, New Brunswick, Canada.

Jug attributed to the Bayley Pottery recovered at the site of Jonathan Lowder's Trading Post in Veazie, Maine, within a circa 1775-1779 archaeological context (courtesy University of Maine).

By 1792, the Bayley Pottery was in decline with Daniel's passing in that year and production ceased altogether when Daniel Bayley Jr. and William Bayley died in 1799. Ideally, this left an opportunity for a potter to fill the demand for red earthenware in the Newburyport area.

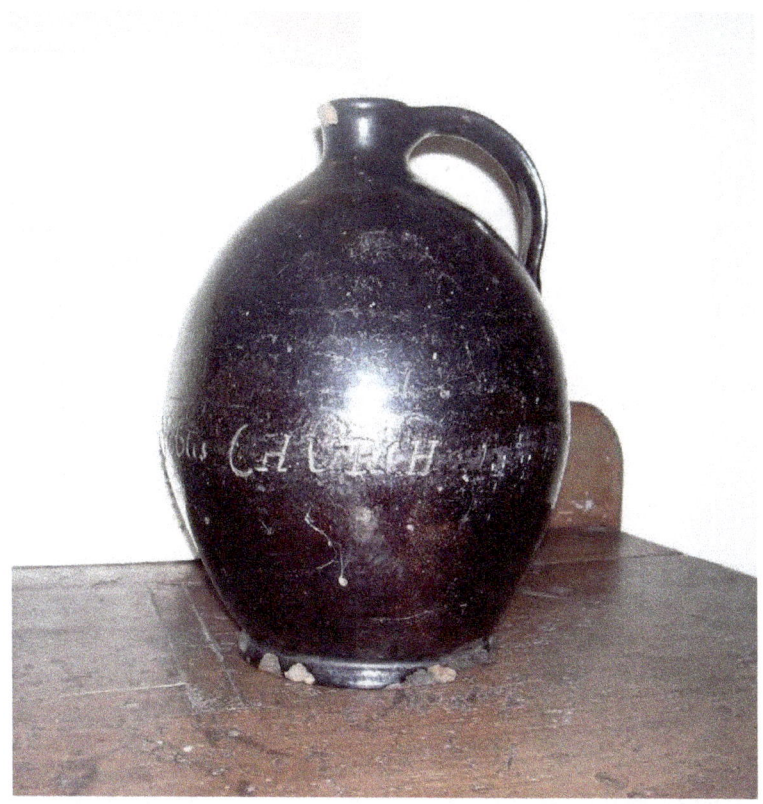

Red earthenware jug manufactured at the Daniel Bayley Pottery, inscribed *"For the use of Mr. Noble's CHURCH July 10, 1763"* (courtesy Museums of Old York).

The William Pecker Pottery

Slip script red earthenware sherds recovered in Historic Westbrook, Maine, possibly made at the Daniel Bayley Pottery, dated "*1770*" (courtesy Matt Anson).

Chamber pot recovered from a circa 1770 context at the site of the Narbonne House in Salem, Mass., attributed to the Daniel Bayley Pottery (courtesy National Park Service).

The William Pecker Pottery

Eighteenth century dish recovered from the bottom of a well in Portsmouth, New Hampshire, possibly made at the Daniel Bayley Pottery (courtesy Louise Richardson).

The William Pecker Pottery

Bowls recovered from the site of the Daniel Bayley Pottery by Lura Woodside Watkins (courtesy National Museum of American History at the Smithsonian Institute).

Bowl sherds recovered from the site of the Daniel Bayley Pottery by Lura Woodside Watkins (courtesy National Museum of American History at the Smithsonian Institute).

The William Pecker Pottery

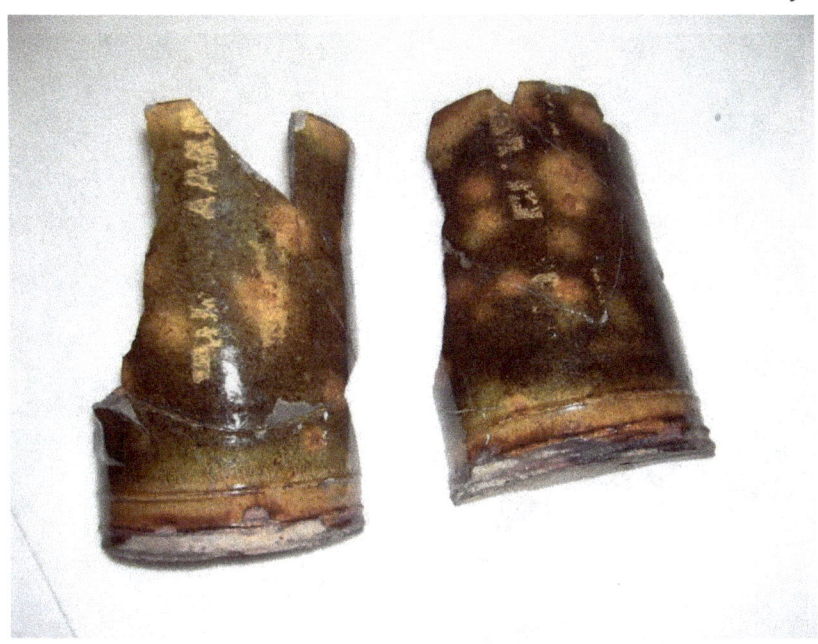

Mugs recovered from the site of the Daniel Bayley Pottery by Lura Woodside Watkins (courtesy National Museum of American History at the Smithsonian Institute).

Incised sherd recovered from the site of the Daniel Bayley Pottery by Lura Woodside Watkins (courtesy National Museum of American History at the Smithsonian Institute).

The William Pecker Pottery

Chamber pot sherds recovered from the site of the Daniel Bayley Pottery by Lura Woodside Watkins (courtesy National Museum of American History at the Smithsonian Institute).

Green glazed sherds recovered from the site of the Daniel Bayley Pottery by Lura Woodside Watkins (courtesy National Museum of American History at the Smithsonian Institute).

Ebenezer Morrison (1741-1803) also operated a business in Newburyport; apparently there was enough demand for multiple businesses, where some of the Bayley family members also worked for Morrison, manufacturing similar forms. Archaeology from the Morrison site can be found today at the National Museum of American History at the Smithsonian Institute.

However, the void left by the Bayley Pottery must have then been largely fulfilled by another local pottery in nearby South Amesbury (Merrimacport), Massachusetts. The wares made in South Amesbury were similar to what was manufactured in Newburyport and Peabody, but it is in this author's opinion that they were more refined. Even more importantly, South Amesbury's production presented an entire new pottery medium not previously produced in Essex County, the production of stoneware in the early nineteenth century.

Eighteenth century mugs attributed to the Bayley family; mug second from right retains a very old note that reads, "*Joseph Bayley Pottery made this mug in Rowley, Mass. before 1735,*" although, it cannot be proven if this was made in Rowley or actually later in the 1700s at the Daniel Bayley Pottery Company.

The William Pecker Pottery

Eighteenth century pans and a jug most likely manufactured in Newburyport found inside the Plumer-Humphries-Barton family estate in Newbury, Mass.

> Chapter 1

South Amesbury's Eighteenth Century Production and the Potters Who Followed

Settled in the northeastern corner of Massachusetts in 1638, South Amesbury (Merrimacport) began as a fishing village along the Merrimack River and was originally a section of Amesbury known as West Amesbury. During the Industrial Revolution, a village developed around the newly formed square in Merrimac, and in 1876, West Amesbury, including Merrimacport (South Amesbury), split from Amesbury, incorporating itself as Merrimac.

Although, long before that happened, South Amesbury was known for its red earthenware production, dating back to the eighteenth century. Known production began before 1775 by Benjamin Bodge (1747-1822) who was born and then baptized in Charlestown, Massachusetts on January 18, 1747. He was likely the nephew of Samuel Bodge, Sr. (1719-1755) who ran a Colonial red earthenware pottery in Charlestown along with his son Samuel Bodge Jr. (1743-1806).

Benjamin married Susanna Pecker (1746-1776) in Haverhill, Massachusetts on September 27, 1770, where he is cited as already being a potter, which would make sense that he had trained or worked in some capacity in Charlestown.

The William Pecker Pottery

The couple's first-born child was John Bodge (1772-1835) who also became a potter, later moving to Fayette, Maine with his father to operate a pottery.

However, records indicate that the couple's daughter Susanna was born in Amesbury on May 6, 1775, which is when his wife died or sometime thereafter. Benjamin married twice more, marrying Sarah Sargent of Amesbury in 1776 and Mehitabel Sheppard of Haverhill in 1781.

Benjamin is first cited as a potter in West Amesbury when he bought land from Enoch Rogers on April 4, 1782. There is no known pottery that can be associated with Bodge's production, although it may appear like the wares manufactured at the Bodge Pottery in Charlestown. Some evidence of this production was recovered in Charlestown by archaeologists in the 1980s as part of Boston's Big Dig project, revealing a wide range of glaze colors, similar to some of the glaze colors known from Merrimacport's nineteenth century production. A notable artifact recovered is the remains of a rim from a jug; the shape of the rim is similar to jugs manufactured in South Amesbury in the late eighteenth and nineteenth century.

Figure 1.1 Jug rim sherd recovered at the site of the Bodge Pottery in Charlestown, Mass. The shape is similar to jugs manufactured in South Amesbury (Merrimacport), Mass. (courtesy City of Boston Archaeology Program).

The William Pecker Pottery

Figure 1.2 (Left) spotted green glazed sherd recovered at the site of the Bodge Pottery in Charlestown, Mass. (courtesy City of Boston Archaeology Program).

Figure 1.3 Various green glazes recovered at the site of the Bodge Pottery in Charlestown, Mass. (courtesy City of Boston Archaeology Program).

The William Pecker Pottery

The most famous of all the potters who worked in Merrimacport is most likely William Pecker (1758-1820), brother of Benjamin Bodge's first wife Susanna. Born in Haverhill on October 10, 1758, Pecker is thought to have trained somewhere in Essex County before he arrived in Merimacport, and is thought to have been working for Benjamin Bodge.

He married Hannah Guile (1765-1828), widow of Major Ezekiel Guile and had one son, Weld Pecker (1802-1869). Weld is described as a *"laborer"* in United States Census Records.

According to Massachusetts author Lura Woodside Watkins' book, *Early New England Potters and Their Wares*, *"The Bodge Pottery continued until the later part of 1791, when its owner, who was then living in Poplin, New Hampshire, sold it (December 5) to Timothy Gordon, a blacksmith. Up to this time, there is no record of Pecker having been a landowner, but in the following year he purchased a lot of some eleven acres on Red Oaks Hill in West Amesbury. Three years later he acquired from Micajah Pillsbury seventeen acres and a dwelling house with another lot of thirty-six acres. His house lot, bordering on the estate of Enoch Rogers, was doubtless in the vicinity."*

Many today think of Pecker as a nineteenth century potter, but his career really began many years earlier and possibly before the American Revolution. He was involved with the eighteenth century potteries as much as he was with those of the nineteenth century. His career was equally divided between two colorfully contrasting times, Colonial and Federal.

But Pecker is best known for his work after 1791, when he ran his own kiln in South Amesbury. It was within this independently run business that his most accomplished wares were produced. The only surviving known piece thought to have been made at the Pecker Pottery in the 1790s is a damaged yellow glazed jug with dripping brown brush strokes. Written across the front in white slip is the date *"1797*. To my

The William Pecker Pottery

knowledge, it is one of only two Pecker jugs with a yellow body glaze, a color not commonly applied on early American red earthenware. Pecker is known for working with a variety of glaze colors, especially on jugs, although he is most known for his orange glazes decorated with dark (manganese) brush strokes. His known forms include handled pots, jars, pitchers, chamber pots, jugs, mugs and flowerpots. He is not known to have worked with much white slip or produced flatware, but archaeology and kiln remains are what would really define the majority of Pecker's work.

Figure 1.4 Eighteenth century red earthenware jug attributed to the William Pecker Pottery in South Amesbury (Merrimacport), Mass. Inscribed in slip "1797" (courtesy Northeast Auctions from the Hilary and Paulette Nolan Collection).

Even though it has not received as much attention in the scholarly world, William Pecker was also a stoneware potter, and ideally, this may be the most important aspect of his production. Previous to this book and a research article I wrote for the August 2015 edition of the *New England Antiques Journal*, titled, "William Pecker: a forgotten stoneware potter from Merrimacport, Mass.," the only other material written on the subject is an academic article written by John Kille for the 2004 issue of *Ceramics in America*, titled, "William Pecker Jar." That jar was found at a Kentucky flea market; it is slumped on one side from a kiln accident and stamped with a bird and flower. Ever since reading that initial article, I have been fascinated with the idea of Pecker's stoneware work. Where did he learn to produce stoneware seeing that it requires a hotter kiln temperature and a different type of clay? He had to have been taught the proper kiln technique to manufacture stoneware; Frederick Carpenter (d. 1827) was producing stoneware in Charlestown during this period, and some of his known production appears like that manufactured by Pecker – Pecker's production may also relate to what was produced in Manhattan in New York City, and in many ways the epicenter for stoneware production in America during this period.

Interestingly, a potter by the name of *"William Pecker"* is thought to have been working in New York City during the 1802-1807 period (Ketchum Jr. *Potters and Potteries of New York State, 1650-1900: Second Edition.* 1987). I have not found any evidence to support this being the same William Pecker from South Amesbury, but his stoneware production in South Amesbury is thought to date from the circa 1810 period. Even though, more importantly, Pecker regularly advertises his pottery business, outhouse and land as being for sale in 1802 in the *Newburyport Gazette*, which is the same year that his name is cited as being in New York City.

The most significant example of Pecker's stoneware production known to exist today is a monumental six-gallon cobalt decorated handled jar, decorated on each side with a stamped bird and a stamped flower. Within the center of each flower is an impressed seal of George Washington, one side has an additional Washington impression and inscribed with the initials "*S.H.*" It is currently unknown who the initials represent.

> FOR SALE, 
>
> A Convenient new two-story House, Barn, Out-Houses, and Potter's works, with about one acre of Land, on which they Stand; laying on the banks of the Merrimack, in Amesbury, commodious for a country seat, or convenient for a mechanical stand. —ALSO—
>
> 30 acres of excellent Land, within a mile of the above premises. For particulars apply to   WILLIAM PECKER, on said Premises ——Amesbury, June 22.
>
> N. B. *A pew and an half in the meetinghouse, in said parish will be sold also.*

Figure 1.5 William Pecker advertising his pottery business and other assets for sale in the *Newburyport Herald & Country Gazette* on Friday June 22, 1802.

Only a small group of stoneware objects manufactured at the Pecker Pottery are known to exist today – the forms include one, two and three gallon jugs in a variety of forms and multiple types of jars. Aside from the bird and flower stamps, a fish stamp was also applied on some stoneware. There are some pieces known to exist with a similar fish stamp, but the only fish stamp positively attributed to the Pecker Pottery is an unmarked jar decorated with Pecker's known bird stamp.

The William Pecker Pottery

Figure 1.6 Monumental six-gallon stoneware jar made at the William Pecker Pottery decorated on both sides with a stamped bird and flower, as well as three impressed seals of George Washington and inscribed with the initial "S.H." (courtesy Crocker Farm Auctions of American Redware and Stoneware.

Figure 1.7 The bird and flower stamps applied at the William Pecker Pottery.

Figure 1.8 The fish stamp applied at the William Pecker Pottery.

Figure 1.9 Two-gallon stoneware jar made at the William Pecker Pottery impressed with a bird and fish stamp (courtesy Crocker Farm Auctions of American Redware and Stonware).

Figure 1.10 William Pecker Jar published in the 2004 issue of *Ceramics in America* (courtesy Bill Chapman).

Among the potters who worked at the Pecker Pottery was James Chase (1779-1849) – he was the son of Pecker's sister Hannah and Edmund Chase, born in West Amesbury on April 9, 1779. He married Olive Lucas of Charlestown when he was thirty-two years old.

James had been training under Pecker for a number of years and had likely learned all of Pecker's secrets in the potter's trade. He saw how Pecker ran the pottery business; he witnessed Pecker's skill on the wheel and how he operated a kiln; he must have known his glaze recipes; and he probably even understood Pecker's wonderful eye for proportion within a perfectly balanced form.

William Pecker died an untimely death. His kiln collapsed on top of him on November 22, 1820. It was a tragic event that cut short the life of a potter who had a lot left to offer his family and many more accomplishments to achieve within the American utilitarian pottery industry.

Pecker's talent was equal to all the best seventeenth, eighteenth and nineteenth century potters working in New England. Pecker was his own business, but he was also a member of an active community of potters working in coastal Massachusetts, who influenced each other through glaze, decoration and form. Fortunately, Pecker's craft did not fade away with his death, and he had a successful pottery to bequeath. With Pecker's passing, James Chase eventually moved the Merrimacport kiln to his property along the Merrimack River, although the remains of this business do not exist today.

In the collection of the National Museum of American History at the Smithsonian Institute in Washington, D.C. are four examples of red earthenware collected by Lura Woodside Watkins in Merrimacport. Each piece is attributed to the James Chase Pottery.

The William Pecker Pottery

> ESSEX, ss. At a Court of Probate holden at Newburyport, in and for said county, on the last Tuesday in March, A. D. 1820. On the petition of Hannah Pecker, administratrix of the estate of WILLIAM PECKER, late of Amesbury in said county, yeoman, deceased, inteftate, shewing that the debts against the estate of said deceased amount to six hundred eighty nine dollars, thirty seven cents more than all his personal estate; and praying, that she may be duly empowered and licensed to sell so much of the real estate of said deceased as shall be necessary for the payment of said debts, with incidental charges:—
>
> Ordered, that the third Tuesday in April next, eleven of the clock before noon, be assigned as the time for considering said petition, at a Court of probate then to be holden at Haverhill, in said county; & that said administratrix give notice to all persons interested, by causing an attested copy of this order to be published three weeks successively before said time in the Newburyport Herald, printed in Newburyport, that they may be present, and shew cause, if any they have, why the prayer of said petition should not be granted.
> D. A. WHITE, Judge of Probate.
> A true copy of record. Attest,
> NATH'L LORD, Jr. Register.
> March 30   q

Figure 1.11 Notice for William Pecker's estate in the *Newburyport Herald* on March 30, 1821.

> NOTICE
> IS hereby given, that the Subscriber has been duly appointed administrator de bonis non of the estate of
> WILLIAM PECKER,
> late of Amesbury, in the county of Essex, yeoman, deceased, and has taken upon himself that trust, by giving bonds as the law directs. All persons having demands upon the estate of said deceased, are required to exhibit the same; and all persons indebted to said estate are called upon to make to
> STEPHEN SARGENT, jr. Adm'r.
> Amesbury, Oct. 7.   q

Figure 1.12 Notice for William Pecker's estate in the *Newburyport Herald* on October 7, 1828.

The William Pecker Pottery

Figure 1.13 Pitcher attributed to the James Chase Pottery in South Amesbury (Merrimacport), Mass.; Lura Woodside Watkins Collection (courtesy National Museum of American History at the Smithsonian Institute).

Figure 1.14 Handled pot attributed to the James Chase Pottery in South Amesbury (Merrimacport), Mass.; Lura Woodside Watkins Collection (courtesy National Museum of American History at the Smithsonian Institute).

The William Pecker Pottery

Figure 1.15 Handled pot attributed to the James Chase Pottery in South Amesbury (Merrimacport), Mass.; Lura Woodside Watkins Collection (courtesy National Museum of American History at the Smithsonian Institute).

Figure 1.16 Bowl attributed to the James Chase Pottery in South Amesbury (Merrimacport), Mass.; Lura Woodside Watkins Collection (courtesy National Museum of American History at the Smithsonian Institute).

It also has to be taken into consideration that some of the forms and possibly even the glazes manufactured at the James Chase Pottery may mimic styles produced at the William Pecker Pottery. For instance, the ribbed extruded handles at both companies are very similar. Although, I was really surprised a few years ago after purchasing a jug that appeared to be produced at the Pecker Pottery, but it was dated twice on the base in pencil "*1836*." As interesting as this is, there is no way to accurately prove if this date coincides with the manufacture of this jug, but it is unquestionably noteworthy.

Figure 1.17 South Amesbury jug inscribed on the base twice in pencil "*1836*."

South Amesbury's pottery tradition did not end when James Chase died in 1849. His son, Phineas Chase (1820-1911) had learned the trade from his father much like James had been taught by his uncle William Pecker. About 1851, he moved the business to the property of a house he had built a short distance from the Merrrimack River, heading towards the square in Merrimac. It has been previously published that little production

The William Pecker Pottery

took place in South Amesbury (Merrimacport) after the 1860s, however, archaeological evidence proves differently, showing that Phineas Chase operated a thriving red earthenware company into the 1880s. An 1884 map of Merrimacport also reveals a brick kiln on the property owned by William Chase along the Merrimack River; William was another son of James Chase.

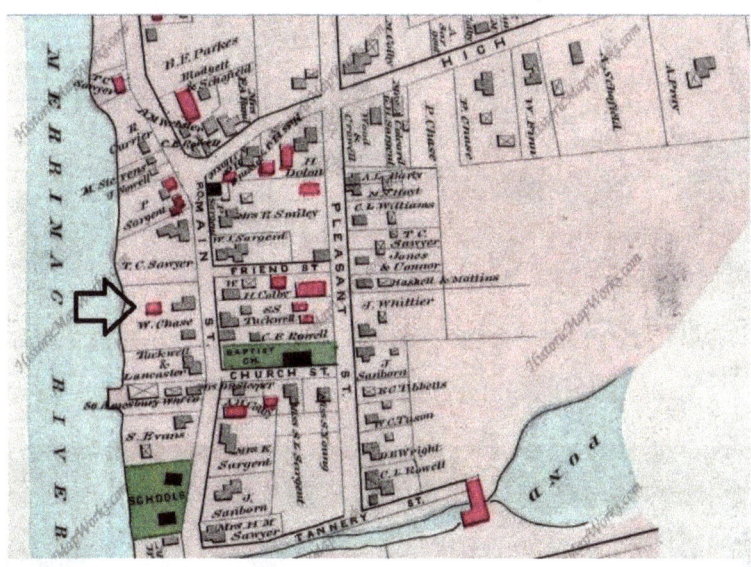

Figure 1.18 1884 map showing the location of William Chase's kiln.

Figure 1.19 Vase possibly made in Merrimacport; found in Haverhill, Mass. (courtesy private collection).

The known forms from the Phineas Chase Pottery include flowerpots and vases, but traditional forms were also manufactured, such as a variety of pots only glazed on the interior. A variety of these type of pots made by the Chases are on permanent display inside a glass case in the lobby of the Merrimac Town Hall.

The William Pecker Pottery

Figure 1.20 Collection of Chase Pottery on display in Merrimac's Town Hall.

Figure 1.21 Photocopy of a billhead from the Phineas Chase Pottery.

The William Pecker Pottery

Figure 1.22 Handled pot possibly made in South Amesbury (Merrimacport), Mass. Found locally in the Newburyport, Mass. area; ht. 6 ¼".

Phineas Chase closed his red earthenware company long before his death in 1911, but when production ceased, more than a century of production in South Amesbury (Merrimacport) ended with it. His obituary read in part, *"Mr. Chase was aged 90 years, 11 months and 16 days. He was a man of sterling honesty and marked integrity and had the respect of the community."*

Working with the current property owners, we have been able to recover some archaeological evidence from the Phineas Chase Pottery, including a wide assortment of glaze colors, such as a great green glaze and various mottled glazes. Archaeology was also conducted on this site in the 1970s by a student from Boston University.

The William Pecker Pottery

Figure 1.23 My nephew Jason and niece Alexis with artifacts collected at the site of the Phineas Chase Pottery in Merrimacport, Mass.

Figure 1.24 Kiln furniture collected at the site of the Phineas Chase Pottery in Merrimacport, Mass.

The William Pecker Pottery

Figure 1.25 Various artifacts collected at the site of the Phineas Chase Pottery in Merrimacport, Mass.

Figure 1.26 Various artifacts collected at the site of the Phineas Chase Pottery in Merrimacport, Mass.

The William Pecker Pottery

Figure 1.27 Mottled green glaze recovered at the site of the Phineas Chase Pottery in Merrimacport, Mass.

Figure 1.28 Green glaze recovered at the site of the Phineas Chase Pottery in Merrimacport, Mass.

The William Pecker Pottery

Figure 1.29 (Top and Bottom) Green glaze recovered at the site of the Phineas Chase Pottery in Merrimacport, Mass.

The William Pecker Pottery

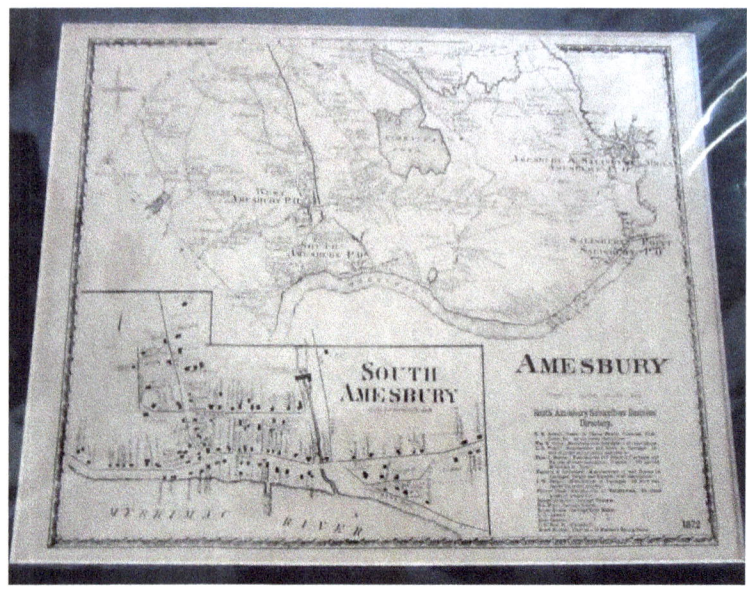

Figure 1.30 1872 Map of South Amesbury (Merrimacport), Mass. showing the location of the Phineas Chase Pottery.

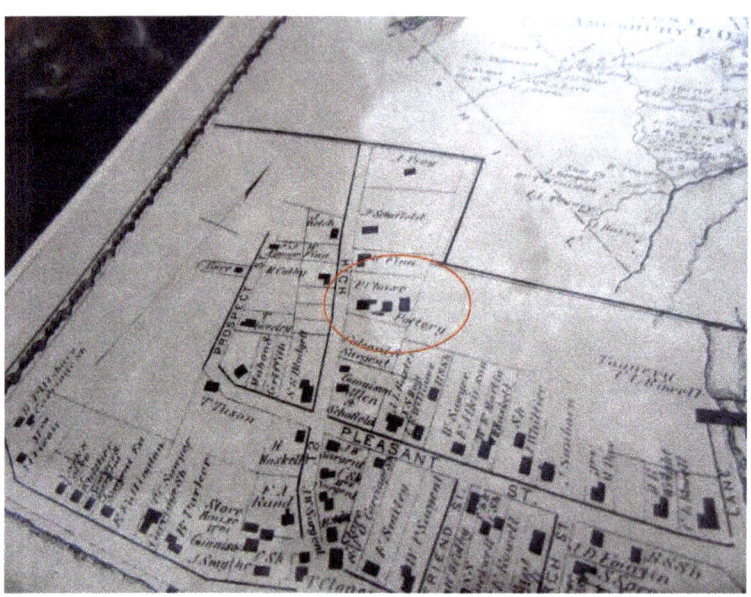

> Chapter 2

The Site of the William Pecker Pottery

In July of 2013, my nephew, Jason, and I left for a bike ride from my Newburyport, Massachusetts home with a specific destination in mind. He had asked if we could go to a place we had never ridden before and I had been lately considering exploring Merrimacport.

I wanted to get a feel for the village, taking a better look where William Pecker lived and worked. I had been imagining for sometime that there must be evidence of Pecker's pottery production somewhere along the Merrimack River. What if we found some?

The six-mile bike ride took us through Amesbury, Merrimac and into Merrimacport, much of it alongside the picturesque Merrimack River with its breathtaking views. This was the same river Pecker most likely used to ship some of his earthenware to the east and west for distribution to places like Newburyport and Haverhill. We rode up hills and down hills – and believe me when I tell you that Jason would rather not have had to struggle riding up any of the steep hills. The day was perfect – blue skies and temperatures in the low 80s with very little humidity.

In Merrimacport, we saw an eighteenth century house with a sign that hung next to the front door that read *"The Potter's House, Circa 1776,"* and a town owned historic park that borders it.

The William Pecker Pottery

The Potter's House and park backup to the Merrimack River. Jason and I peered down onto the river's shore. There was a cliff and it dropped directly down. I did not expect to see much. Fortunately, it was low tide, and as we both looked down, we saw bricks – in fact, an unexpected amount of bricks that were certainly out of place this far up river. Bricks are often seen on the shores of Newburyport, a few miles downriver, where they came as ballast in ships from England and were used to rebuild the downtown area after the great fire of 1811. There was no apparent reason why so many were on the shores of Merrimacport and largely only in this one location.

As any curious nine-year old boy would do, Jason scrambled down to the shore, and after only a few minutes, yelled for me to come down and see what he had found. I could hear the excitement in his voice. He kept yelling for me.

When I got there, he held up a crooked burnt looking brick and asked what it was. That got me as excited as he was – it appeared to be a kiln brick. Could it possibly have been part of William Pecker's kiln or perhaps from one operated by the Chase family?

Looking around, I saw bricks surrounded us: burnt and deformed bricks lay all over the shore. Some even retained bits and pieces of red earthenware that adhered to them, while some of the others were partly covered in glaze. Some bricks were just burnt and deformed so I also wondered whether they were manufacturing bricks in Merrimacport.

The steep ledge above the bricks had been eroded by storms. The root system of half a dozen or so trees had been exposed and among them a number of bricks could be seen poking out. Although, of all the artifacts, the most intriguing may have been a deformed brick that stood alone in the mud. It was still wet from the receding tide. It glistened in the sunlight and made me think of William Pecker and his pottery.

Jason and I continued to periodically visit this site, however, our most important discovery happened the following summer. Out of mere curiosity, we investigated a few hundred yards upriver from our initial discovery. I am not sure why, but I had a gut instinct that we would find something there. We were in search of any red earthenware remains from Pecker or the businesses that predated or followed him after his death in 1820.

The two of us climbed carefully down a steep hill that recent erosion had transformed from a sloping hillside into a cliff. Our way down was hampered by thick brush that made us both victims of vicious thorns. The cliff ended on the shore of the Merrimack River. This area is completely covered with water at high tide, but at low tide there is a large stretch of beach.

On this particular day, it was mid-tide, so there was a small area of beach to walk around. We saw all sorts of green plant life from the river that covered the rock-lined shore. It was also littered with all sorts of debris from old logs and trees; however, that is not all we saw.

A number of mature tree branches full of green leaves hung over the brackish water that made for a beautiful setting. It reminded me of some of the lakes in Maine that I used to vacation at with my family as a kid. As I looked up the hill, I imagined William Pecker's pottery business that once peered down at where I was standing.

I was amazed to find dozens and dozens of stoneware sherds at the base of the cliff. The forms I have been able to identify since first discovering this area are crocks, jars and jugs; there may be other forms, but unfortunately, I am not yet able to prove that. There was also an abundance of stoneware kiln furniture and even slightly oversized and oddly shaped bricks. I was astonished that such important historical artifacts with substantial information were lying in plain sight, yet unnoticed.

It appears that Pecker owned a large stretch of land that ran adjacent to the Merrimack River – and the furthest point west may have been the location where he manufactured stoneware. My basis for this interpretation is due to the amount of stoneware evidence we found that is not visible anywhere else in Merrimacport today.

There was a small stretch, probably twenty-five yards wide, where all of the artifacts and sherds appeared. We have been routinely visiting this site ever since, and as a result, we can clearly see a variety of stoneware styles that Pecker used in his production, such as exterior glaze treatments, interior glazes, handles and a variety forms like multiple types of jugs. Some of the sherds were decorated with cobalt and some were not. We also found plenty of kiln furniture.

All of the artifacts seemed to have been exposed from the hill that we had climbed down, which had been battered by storms, but I also question whether Pecker discarded some of his kiln waste directly into the Merrimack River.

The stoneware sherds were found mixed in with a variety of red earthenware sherds, most of which appeared to be from thickly potted utilitarian pots, although we did discover some sherds in the form of known Pecker Pottery red earthenware jugs. Interestingly, most of the red earthenware glazes were colors I have never seen attributed to Merrimacport.

As we continued to look around, the bright summer sunlight sparkled on a sherd mixed in with green sea grass a few inches below the surface of the Merrimack River. We both stood silently peering down into the warm calm water. We could see directly to the sandy and muddy bottom. The water was crystal clear; small fish were swimming near what appeared to be a stoneware sherd. I was really in awe of what I saw. I quickly pulled the sherd out of the water and showed it to my nephew as water dripped from it with a familiar decoration.

We had found an unbelievable artifact! It was partially covered in cobalt and stamped with the same bird motif as was the crock discovered at a Kentucky flea market and written about in the 2004 issue of *Ceramics in America*. Nearly ten years later, we found archaeological evidence at the site of the Pecker Pottery about the stoneware jar that was part of the reason I had so much interest to begin with in William Pecker's production. What are the chances of that happening!

To date, my nephew, my niece Alexis and myself have found hundreds of stoneware sherds and a lot of kiln furniture. There is no doubt that Pecker was not only an incredibly talented red earthenware potter, but he was also a stoneware potter. Because of this early date of production for both types of pottery, Pecker may have only been the second potter in New England successfully producing red earthenware and stoneware;

The William Pecker Pottery

the other being the Parker Pottery in Charlestown, Massachusetts in the 1740s. It is quite an accomplishment that has been in some ways overlooked through the years.

Figure 2.1 Stoneware sherd decorated with a bird motif that I found with my nephew sitting among sea grass in the Merrimack River.

The William Pecker Pottery

Figure 2.2 My nephew looking out at the area where William Pecker operated a pottery along the Merrimack River in South Amesbury (Merrimacport), Mass., circa 1791-1820.

Figure 2.3 The area where William Pecker operated a pottery along the Merrimack River in South Amesbury (Merrimacport), Mass., circa 1791-1820.

The William Pecker Pottery

Figure 2.4 The area where William Pecker operated a pottery along the Merrimack River in South Amesbury (Merrimacport), Mass., circa 1791-1820.

Figure 2.5 The area where William Pecker operated a pottery along the Merrimack River in South Amesbury (Merrimacport), Mass., circa 1791-1820.

> Chapter 3

South Amesbury's Red Earthenware and Archaeology

The red earthenware archaeological evidence recovered at the site of the William Pecker Pottery in South Amesbury has yielded a wide range of artifacts, like kiln furniture and thousands of sherds. The site is part of an ongoing investigation; the recovered forms include a wide range of utilitarian pots unglazed on the exterior and either glazed or unglazed on the interior. Many are adorned in dark glazes like brown and black or more vibrant colors such as greens, raspberry, orange, cream and even a gold color. A number of pieces of milk pans have also been found, similar in form to pans manufactured in places like Maine, where there was a thriving dairy industry in the nineteenth century. Other notable recovered artifacts include mugs and jugs, along with handles that could have gone to a number of handled forms.

Figure 3.1 Red earthenware kiln furniture recovered in South Amesbury (Merrimacport), Mass.

The William Pecker Pottery

Figure 3.2 My niece Alexis with red earthenware sherds recovered in South Amesbury (Merrrimacport), Mass.

Figure 3.3 Colorfully glazed red earthenware sherds recovered in South Amesbury (Merrimacport), Mass.

The William Pecker Pottery

Figure 3.4 Colorfully glazed red earthenware sherd recovered in South Amesbury (Merrimacport), Mass.

Figure 3.5 Remains of a red earthenware mug recovered in South Amesbury (Merrimacport), Mass.

The William Pecker Pottery

Figure 3.6 Some of the kiln bricks recovered in South Amesbury (Merrimacport), Mass.

Figure 3.7a Red earthenware kiln furniture recovered in South Amesbury (Merrimacport), Mass.

The William Pecker Pottery

Figure 3.7b Red earthenware kiln furniture recovered in South Amesbury (Merrimacport), Mass.

Figure 3.7c Red earthenware kiln furniture recovered in South Amesbury (Merrimacport), Mass.

Figure 3.8a Examples of utilitarian pots recovered in South Amesbury (Merrimacport), Mass.

Figure 3.8b The interior of those pots, some are glazed and some are unglazed.

The William Pecker Pottery

Figure 3.9a Black glazed red earthenware jug manufactured in South Amesbury (Merrimacport), Mass. with the base of a matching jug recovered at the site of the William Pecker Pottery.

Figure 3.9b Comparing both bases.

The William Pecker Pottery

Figure 3.10 Black glazed red earthenware jug manufactured in South Amesbury (Merrimacport), Mass. with a matching handle sherd recovered at the site of the William Pecker Pottery.

The William Pecker Pottery

Figure 3.11 Black glazed red earthenware jug manufactured in South Amesbury (Merrimacport), Mass. with another matching handle sherd recovered at the site of the William Pecker Pottery.

The William Pecker Pottery

Figure 3.12a Red earthenware jug from South Amesbury (Merrimacport), Mass. with a matching glazed jug sherd recovered in South Amesbury. The form and decoration on this jug appear like William Pecker's production, although the base is dated twice in pencil "1836." It is possible that much of James Chase's production appeared like that made at the William Pecker pottery seeing that Chase trained and worked with Pecker.

Figure 3.12b The base of the jug is dated twice in pencil "1836."

> Chapter 4

South Amesbury's Stoneware and Archaeology

For years, there has been a lot of speculation behind a small group of stoneware objects marked *"Wm PECKER."* Most notably, the 2004 issue of *Ceramics in America* presented a jar discovered at a Kentucky flea market to an international audience, bringing a great deal of interest and the meaning behind this object, more specifically, its origin and where exactly it was manufactured.

It is because of this article that I began investigating Merrimacport for any evidence of William Pecker's stoneware production. I really had no idea where to look, however my gut instinct and a lot of luck helped identify some of the surviving remains from William Pecker's stoneware kiln.

This type of evidence has never been presented in publication before, revealing that William Pecker was not only a red earthenware potter in South Amesbury, but he also transformed himself into a stoneware potter in the early nineteenth century.

Recovered evidence includes dozens of examples of kiln furniture, many of which are whole and reveal finger impressions and finger prints by whom they were made. Other notable artifacts present various types of exterior glaze treatments, along with interiors that are either left unglazed or decorated with a salt glaze or a brown slip. A number of different handles were recovered, along with rims, bases, wasters and even the remains of saggars. This is all conclusive

The William Pecker Pottery

evidence that William Pecker was undoubtedly manufacturing stoneware in South Amesbury, perhaps about the circa 1810 period. Although, it is unknown if there were other potters involved with this production at the William Pecker Pottery.

The forms include the remains of multiple styles of jugs and various types of jars. It is certainly possible that additional shapes were manufactured, but there is no evidence to support that idea. Some of the jugs and jars are similar to styles manufactured during the same period in places like Charlestown, Massachusetts, Connecticut, Manhattan (New York City) and New Jersey.

It is currently unknown where William Pecker acquired the clay used to manufacture stoneware. The clay beds in Merrimacport are suitable for lower fired red earthenware production, although the clays used for stoneware would have been imported, possibly from the same source that was used in at the Frederick Carpenter Pottery in Charlestown.

Pecker also produced some stoneware with cobalt, but it was usually applied in sparing amounts, whether it was used around handle terminals, highlighting his *"Wm PECKER"* mark or highlighting his stamped bird, fish and flower design.

Aside from the kiln production remains (furniture and saggars), the most significant discovery may be the remains of Pecker's bird motif that was discovered in four sherds in the same area of Merrimacport on separate occasions. This is the same bird found on the jar discovered at the Kentucky flea market, as well as a few other significant pieces known to exist today.

Figure 4.1 Early nineteenth century two-gallon stoneware jugs attributed to the Frederick Carpenter Pottery in Charlestown, Mass. Each is impressed *"BOSTON."*

Figure 4.2 My niece Alexis with some stoneware sherds from the William Pecker Pottery discovered in South Amesbury (Merrimacport), Mass.

Figure 4.3 My niece Alexis with a stoneware sherd from the William Pecker Pottery discovered in South Amesbury (Merrimacport), Mass.

The William Pecker Pottery

Figure 4.4a My niece Alexis with stoneware kiln furniture from the William Pecker Pottery recovered in South Amesbury (Merrimacport), Mass.

Figure 4.4b Stoneware kiln furniture from the William Pecker Pottery.

The William Pecker Pottery

Figure 4.5a Stoneware kiln furniture from the William Pecker Pottery recovered in South Amesbury (Merrimacport), Mass.

Figure 4.5b Stoneware kiln furniture from the William Pecker Pottery recovered in South Amesbury (Merrimacport), Mass.

The William Pecker Pottery

Figure 4.5c Stoneware kiln furniture from the William Pecker Pottery recovered in South Amesbury (Merrimacport), Mass.

Figure 4.5d Stoneware kiln furniture from the William Pecker Pottery recovered in South Amesbury (Merrimacport), Mass.

Figure 4.6a Various stoneware sherds from the William Pecker Pottery with brown slip decorated interiors.

Figure 4.6b Brown slip decorated interiors.

The William Pecker Pottery

Figure 4.7a Stoneware sherd from the William Pecker Pottery left unglazed on the interior.

Figure 4.7b Unglazed on the interior.

The William Pecker Pottery

Figure 4.8a Stoneware sherds from the William Pecker Pottery decorated with a salt glaze on both the exterior and interior.

Figure 4.8b Salt glazed interiors.

Figure 4.9a Stoneware bases from the William Pecker Pottery.

Figure 4.9b Stoneware bases from the William Pecker Pottery.

The William Pecker Pottery

Figure 4.9c Stoneware bases from the William Pecker Pottery.

Figure 4.10a Stoneware handles and handle terminals from the William Pecker Pottery.

The William Pecker Pottery

Figure 4.10b Stoneware handles and handle terminals from the William Pecker Pottery.

Figure 4.10c Stoneware handles and handle terminals from the William Pecker Pottery.

The William Pecker Pottery

Figure 4.11 Incised stoneware sherds from the William Pecker Pottery.

Figure 4.12 Cobalt decorated sherds from the William Pecker Pottery.

Figure 4.13 Various exterior glaze treatments on stoneware from the William Pecker Pottery.

Figure 4.14 Stoneware rims from the William Pecker Pottery.

The William Pecker Pottery

Figure 4.15a Stoneware artifacts from the William Pecker Pottery.

Figure 4.15b Stoneware artifacts from the William Pecker Pottery.

The William Pecker Pottery

Figure 4.16 Remains of a stoneware stamped cobalt decorated bird from the William Pecker Pottery; stamps of a fish and a flower were also used at the Pecker Pottery.

Figure 4.17 Remains of a narrow stoneware jug from the William Pecker Pottery.

The William Pecker Pottery

Figure 4.18a Comparison of the stamped cobalt decorated bird sherds to an existing William Pecker Pottery jar adorned with the same bird (the other side of the jar is stamped with a fish).

The William Pecker Pottery

Figure 4.18b Comparison of the sherd with the bird's head.

Figure 4.18c Comparison of the sherd with the bird's tail.

The William Pecker Pottery

Figure 4.19a Existing jar marked "Wm PECKER" next to the remains of a similar shaped jug recovered at the site of the William Pecker Pottery.

Figure 4.19b A similar shaped red earthenware jug from South Amesbury (Merrimacport), Mass.

The William Pecker Pottery

Figure 4.20a Existing two gallon stoneware jug marked "Wm PECKER" with a very similar rim and handle artifact recovered at the site of the William Pecker Pottery. Note the matching two-gallon capacity mark.

Figure 4.20b Existing Two gallon stoneware jug marked "Wm PECKER" with a very similar rim and handle artifact recovered at the site of the William Pecker Pottery. Note the matching use of cobalt.

The William Pecker Pottery

Figure 4.21 Kiln furniture mark on the base of a two gallon stoneware jug marked "Wm PECKER;" along with a piece of kiln furniture recovered at the site of the William Pecker Pottery.

> Chapter 5

William Pecker's Exports and Museum Collections

The wares manufactured in South Amesbury (Merrimacport) have been recovered in various early contexts in the Newburyport and Amesbury area, Haverhill, Massachusetts, as well as southern New Hampshire. Most notably are a group of objects illustrated in Lura Woodside Watkins' book *Early New England Potters and Their Wares* (figures 40, 41 and 58), now in the collections of the National Museum of American History at the Smithsonian Institute in Washington, D.C. and Old Sturbridge Village in Sturbridge, Massachusetts. There is no evidence to suggest that William Pecker's production traveled in large amounts to the south of the Newburyport area since so much pottery was produced in that area by the prolific potters working at the industry in South Danvers (Peabody).

However, in the past ten years, I have studied two jugs of particular interest that appear like they were manufactured at the Pecker Pottery, both of which retain important histories of ownership.

The first jug (figures 5.2a and 5.2b) is a classic style that was manufactured at the William Pecker Pottery, circa 1791-1820. It is decorated in Pecker's signature orange glaze with dark bush strokes of manganese.

Gorham, Maine historian Chris Havey discovered the jug in the 1990s; it was found beneath a building that was taken down on the property of a late eighteenth century house in historic Westbrook, Maine, a neighboring community of Portland,

The William Pecker Pottery

Maine. There is no evidence to support it, but it is possible that this jug was shipped to Portland, and then made its way into Westbrook.

The jug was found alongside other New England red earthenware: a nineteenth century southern Maine jug (figure 5.3), a large flowerpot with a painted gold stripe below the rim, possibly from the Moses Paige Pottery in Peabody, Massachusetts after 1875 (figure 5.4) and a hanging flower from the late 1800s possibly from Maine (figures 5.5a and 5.5b)

The second jug (figure 5.6) closely resembles production in Merrimacport, but it may also be from New Hampshire or even Maine, where there was some similar production. The jug was found in an early family context of ownership in Sandwich, New Hampshire, a small community nestled between the state's lakes region and the White Mountain National Forest. It was discovered alongside other types of northern New England red earthenware, such as jugs, pans and utilitarian pots.

Other than these early contexts, Merrimacport pottery is also represented in major museum collections around the country, including the Smithsonian, Old Sturbridge Village, Winterthur Museum, Historic Deerfield, the Museum of Fine Arts, Boston, Strawbery Banke Museum, the Museum of Old Newbury, Historic New England and the John Ashley House in Sheffield, Massachusetts, among others.

Figure 5.1 Three pieces of South Amesbury (Merrimacport), Mass. pottery on display in the Ashley House in Sheffield, Mass. (courtesy Ashley House).

The William Pecker Pottery

Figure 5.2a William Pecker Pottery Pottery jug recovered in Historic Westbrok, Maine (courtesy Chris Havey).

Figure 5.2b Interior of the jug remains (courtesy Chris Havey).

The William Pecker Pottery

Figure 5.3 Southern Maine jug recovered in Historic Westbrook, Maine alongside the William Pecker Pottery jug (courtesy Chris Havey).

Figure 5.4 Flowerpot likely from the Moses Paige Pottery in Peabody, Mass. recovered alongside the William Pecker Pottery jug in Historic Westbrook, Maine (courtesy Chris Havey).

The William Pecker Pottery

Figure 5.5a Likely Maine flowerpot recovered in Historic Westbrook, Maine alongside the William Pecker Pottery jug (courtesy Chris Havey).

Figure 5.5b Base of the flowerpot (courtesy Chris Havey).

The William Pecker Pottery

Figure 5.6 Red earthenware jug possibly made in South Amesbury (Merrimacport), Mass. that retains an early history of ownership in Sandwich, New Hampshire.

The William Pecker Pottery

The remains of a mug (figure 5.7) is also a notable discovery recovered at an eighteenth century home located at 87 Washington Street in the historic district in Marblehead, Massachusetts. This sherd may be from South Danvers (Peabody), but it also closely resembles production from the William Pecker Pottery. It is shown with a mug to the right made at the Pecker Pottery and a coastal Massachusetts jug in the background.

Figure 5.7 (Front left) Red earthenware sherd recovered on the property of an eighteenth century house in the historic district in Marblehead, Mass. Manufactured in either South Danvers (Peabody), Mass. or at the William Pecker Pottery in South Amesbury, Mass. (courtesy Jim Laverdiere).

> Chapter 6

William Pecker's Legacy

William Pecker's skill is somewhat unique for some American utilitarian potters around the turn of the nineteenth century. It appears that he was equally skilled in red earthenware and stoneware production. I can only imagine how his stoneware may have progressed, and possibly even succeeded the red earthenware production, had he not been tragically killed in a kiln accident.

At the time, he must have been aware of the popularity of stoneware within the American marketplace so it is possible that he was attempting to transition his company to include that type of production, a type of production that he could have likely capitalized with in marketplaces in northern Massachusetts, New Hampshire and even Maine. Perhaps, he may have even transformed the company to be more along the lines of the stoneware industry that existed in Charlestown during the period.

Interestingly, though, red earthenware manufactured at the Thomas O'Hara Goodwin (1796-1880) Pottery in West Hartford, Connecticut has been mistaken through the years for wares made at the William Pecker Pottery. The confusion is a result of a nearly identical glaze style, thus proving why the form is so important. Much like Pecker, Goodwin was also a stoneware potter. Similar glazes were also produced in Middlebury, Vermont, southeastern Massachusetts, Norwalk,

Connecticut, Long Island, Pennsylvania, elsewhere in Massachusetts, along with other locations. The reason for the similarities is a result of the common glaze ingredients, usually being lead and manganese.

Figure 6.1 Red earthenware plate inscribed in slip "Thomas/Goodwin/West Hartford" (courtesy Connecticut Historical Society).

The William Pecker Pottery

Figure 6.2 Jars manufactured by Thomas O'Hara Goodwin in West Hartford, Connecticut; (Left) stamped "T.O. Goodwin" and (Right) Stamped "West Hartford" (courtesy Connecticut Historical Society).

Figure 6.3 Jars attributed to Thomas O'Hara Goodwin in West Hartford, CT.

Figure 6.4 Jars attributed to West Hartford, Connecticut.

Figure 6.5 Incised and slip decorated red earthenware jug likely made in West Hartford; form is similar to stoneware jugs made at the William Pecker Pottery (courtesy Metropolitan Museum of Art).

The William Pecker Pottery

Nevertheless, no matter the pottery medium, William Pecker mastered the craft – and it is even more fascinating that he appears to have conquered the chemistry required to simultaneously manufacture red earthenware and stoneware at the same business. He may have owned two separate kilns or fired both types of wares in the same kiln. Very few potters in New England accomplished the requirements and skill it took to master such a dual craft only a few decades after the American Revolution. It is even more fascinating considering that Pecker was only a country-style potter with possibly less financial resources than many other potters who worked in urban industries in the years around the turn of the nineteenth century. In fact, most of the stoneware production that took place during this period happened in and around urban settings. William Pecker should not only be remembered today for his well-known talent as a red earthenware potter – he should also be remembered for his skill as a stoneware potter.

Figure 6.6 William Pecker's (1758-1820) gravestone in Lower Corner Cemetery in Merrimac, Mass.

> Illustrations

Note: Unless otherwise indicated, all of the red earthenware manufactured in South Amesbury (Merrimacport), Massachusetts is either left unglazed or decorated with a lead glaze, multiple glaze colors and various types of slip decoration. The stoneware is salt glazed on the exterior with either a salt glazed interior, a slip interior or an untreated interior. The majority of these pieces are not signed by the potter, although the few marked pieces are noted.

> Partially Glazed Household Wares

1a) Jar possibly made in South Amesbury (Merrrimacport), Mass. Purchased in Portland, Maine, but it seems like it is related to the jar in picture 2 with a strong context; ht. 9".

1b) View of the interior.

The William Pecker Pottery

2a) Jar found in southern New Hampshire not far from Merrimacport, Mass. The green glazed interior is similar to green glazes manufactured in South Amesbury (Merrimacport); ht. 7 ½".

2b) View of the interior.

The William Pecker Pottery

3a) Large red earthenware pan found in an old house in Merrimacport, Mass. (image courtesy private collection)

3b) View of the pan's base.

The William Pecker Pottery

4) Eighteenth or nineteenth century red earthenware pot dug by my father Richard Thomas at 28 Kent Street in Newburyport, Mass. in 1977; either made at the Bayley Pottery in Newburyport or in South Amesbury (Merrimacport), Mass.

5) Red earthenware flowerpot recovered from the muddy shoreline of the Merrimack River in Newburyport, Mass.; either made in Newburyport or Merrimacport, Mass.

> Glazed Household Wares

6) Red earthenware jug made in South Amesbury (Merrimacport), Mass.; ht. 7 **7/8**".

The William Pecker Pottery

7) Red earthenware jug made in South Amesbury (Merrimacport), Mass. The base is dated twice in pencil "1836," although it is unknown if the date is accurate; ht. 8 ¼".

The William Pecker Pottery

8) Red earthenware jug attributed to the William Pecker Pottery in South Amesbury (Merrimacport), Mass.; ht. 7 ¼".

The William Pecker Pottery

9) Red earthenware jug attributed to the William Pecker Pottery in South Amesbury (Merrimacport), Mass.; ht. 9 ¼".

10) Red earthenware jug attributed to the William Pecker Pottery in South Amesbury (Merrimacport), Mass.; ht. 8 ¾".

The William Pecker Pottery

11) Red earthenware jug attributed to the William Pecker Pottery in South Amesbury (Merrimacport), Mass.; ht. 8 ¾".

12) Red earthenware jug attributed to the William Pecker Pottery in South Amesbury (Merrimacport), Mass.; ht. 8 ¾".

13) Red earthenware jug attributed to the William Pecker Pottery in South Amesbury (Merrimacport), Mass.; ht. 7 ½".

The William Pecker Pottery

14) Red earthenware jug made in South Amesbury (Merrimacport), Mass.; ht. 7 ½".

15) Red earthenware jug made in South Amesbury (Merrimacport), Mass.; ht. 7 ¼".

The William Pecker Pottery

16) Red earthenware jug attributed to the William Pecker Pottery in South Amesbury (Merrimacport), Mass.; ht. 11 ¼".

17) Red earthenware jug attributed to the William Pecker Pottery in South Amesbury (Merrimacport), Mass. (courtesy Jim Laverdiere).

The William Pecker Pottery

18) Reassembled red earthenware jug made at the William Pecker Pottery that was recovered from beneath a house in Historic Westbrook, Maine (courtesy Chris Havey).

19) Red earthenware jug attributed to South Amesbury (Merrimacport), Mass., found in Maine, appears to be filled with maple syrup.

20) Red earthenware jug attributed to the William Pecker Pottery in South Amesbury (Merrimacport), Mass. (courtesy Historic New England).

21) Red earthenware jug attributed to the William Pecker Pottery in South Amesbury (Merrimacport), Mass. (courtesy Skinner, Inc.).

The William Pecker Pottery

22) Red earthenware jug attributed to the William Pecker Pottery in South Amesbury (Merrimacport), Mass. (courtesy Old Sturbridge Village); ht. 7".

23) Red earthenware jug attributed to the William Pecker Pottery in South Amesbury (Merrimacport), Mass. (courtesy National Museum of American History at the Smithsonian Institute); ht. 9 ¼".

The William Pecker Pottery

24a) Red earthenware jug attributed to the William Pecker Pottery in South Amesbury (Merrimacport), Mass. (courtesy National Museum of American History at the Smithsonian Institute).

24b) View of the handle (courtesy National Museum of American History at the Smithsonian Institute).

The William Pecker Pottery

25) (Left) Red earthenware jug from the Howard Gilman Foundation Collection attributed to the William Pecker Pottery in South Amesbury (Merrimacport), Mass. (courtesy Christies).

26) Four Red earthenware jugs attributed to the William Pecker Pottery in South Amesbury (Merrimacport), Mass. The large jar shown on the top row may also be from the Pecker Pottery (courtesy John Sideli).

The William Pecker Pottery

27) Red earthenware jug attributed to the William Pecker Pottery in South Amesbury (Merrimacport), Mass. (courtesy Connecticut Historical Society); ht. 11 3/8".

The William Pecker Pottery

28) Red earthenware jug attributed to the William Pecker Pottery in South Amesbury (Merrimacport), Mass. (courtesy Ron and Penny Dionne Collection).

29) Red earthenware jug attributed to the William Pecker Pottery in South Amesbury (Merrimacport), Mass. (courtesy Historic Deerfield); ht. 10 ¾".

The William Pecker Pottery

30) Red earthenware mug attributed to the William Pecker Pottery in South Amesbury (Merrimacport), Mass.; ht. 5".

31) Red earthenware mug attributed to the William Pecker Pottery in South Amesbury (Merrimacport), Mass.; ht. 4 ¾".

32) Red earthenware mug attributed to the William Pecker Pottery in South Amesbury (Merrimacport), Mass.; ht. 3 5/8".

33) Red earthenware mug attributed to the William Pecker Pottery in South Amesbury (Merrimacport), Mass. (courtesy Ross Levett).

The William Pecker Pottery

34) Red earthenware mug attributed to the William Pecker Pottery in South Amesbury (Merrimacport), Mass. (courtesy Crocker Farm Auctions of American Redware and Stoneware); ht. 6 3/8".

35) Red earthenware pot attributed to the William Pecker Pottery in South Amesbury (Merrimacport), Mass.; ht. 8 7/8"

The William Pecker Pottery

36) Red earthenware pot attributed to the William Pecker Pottery in South Amesbury (Merrimacport), Mass.; ht. 8 ¾".

The William Pecker Pottery

37) Red earthenware pot attributed to the William Pecker Pottery in South Amesbury (Merrimacport), Mass.; ht. 6 7/8"

The William Pecker Pottery

38) Red earthenware pot attributed to the William Pecker Pottery in South Amesbury (Merrimacport), Mass.; ht. 8 ¾".

39) Red earthenware pot attributed to the William Pecker Pottery in South Amesbury (Merrimacport), Mass.; ht. 4 ¾"

40) Red earthenware pot attributed to the William Pecker Pottery in South Amesbury (Merrimacport), Mass.; ht. 6 7/8".

41) Red earthenware pot attributed to South Amesbury (Merrimacport), Mass.; ht. 5 ¼".

42) Red earthenware pot attributed to South Amesbury (Merrimacport), Mass.; ht. 6 ½"

43) Red earthenware pot attributed to the William Pecker Pottery in South Amesbury (Merrimacport), Mass.; ht. 7 ½".

44) Red earthenware pot attributed to South Amesbury (Merrimacport), Mass., probably made at the James Chase Pottery; ht. 8".

45) Red earthenware pot attributed to South Amesbury (Merrimacport), Mass.; ht. 8".

The William Pecker Pottery

46) Red earthenware pot attributed to South Amesbury (Merrimacport), Mass.; ht. 8".

The William Pecker Pottery

47) Red earthenware pitcher attributed to South Amesbury (Merrimacport), Mass.; ht. 6 ½".

The William Pecker Pottery

48) Red earthenware pot attributed to the William Pecker Pottery in South Amesbury (Merrimacport), Mass.; ht. 7 ¾".

The William Pecker Pottery

49) Red earthenware pot attributed to the William Pecker Pottery in South Amesbury (Merrimacport), Mass.; ht. 8 5/8".

50) Red earthenware pot attributed to the William Pecker Pottery in South Amesbury (Merrimacport), Mass.; ht. 7 ½".

The William Pecker Pottery

51) Red earthenware pot attributed to South Amesbury (Merrimacport), Mass., probably made at the William Pecker Pottery; ht. 9".

52) Red earthenware pot attributed to South Amesbury (Merrimacport), Mass.; ht. 8 ¾".

53) Red earthenware pot attributed to South Amesbury (Merrimacport), Mass., probably made at the William Pecker Pottery; ht. 8 ¾".

The William Pecker Pottery

54) Red earthenware pitcher attributed to South Amesbury (Merrimacport), Mass.; ht. 7 ½".

The William Pecker Pottery

55) Red earthenware pot attributed to South Amesbury (Merrimacport), Mass. that I discovered with my niece Alexis in Concord, New Hampshire; ht. 5".

56) Red earthenware pot attributed to the William Pecker Pottery in South Amesbury (Merrimacport), Mass.; ht. 5 ¼".

The William Pecker Pottery

57) Red earthenware pot attributed to the William Pecker Pottery in South Amesbury (Merrimacport), Mass. (courtesy National Museum of American History at the Smithsonian Institute).

The William Pecker Pottery

58) Red earthenware pot attributed to the William Pecker Pottery in South Amesbury (Merrimacport), Mass. (courtesy Sam Herrup).

59) Red earthenware pitcher attributed to the William Pecker Pottery in South Amesbury (Merrimacport), Mass. (courtesy Charlie Huntress).

The William Pecker Pottery

60) Red earthenware pot attributed to South Amesbury (Merrimacport), Mass. (courtesy Strawbery Banke).

61) Red earthenware pitcher and pot attributed to the William Pecker Pottery in South Amesbury (Merrimacport), Mass. (courtesy Museum of Old Newbury).

The William Pecker Pottery

62) Red earthenware pot attributed to South Amesbury (Merrimacport), Mass. (courtesy private collection).

63) Red earthenware pot attributed to the William Pecker Pottery in South Amesbury (Merrimacport), Mass. (courtesy Bennington Museum); ht. 7 ½".

The William Pecker Pottery

64) Red earthenware pot attributed to the William Pecker Pottery in South Amesbury (Merrimacport), Mass. (courtesy Anthony Butera Jr.); ht. 5".

65) Red earthenware pot attributed to the William Pecker Pottery in South Amesbury (Merrimacport), Mass. (courtesy private collection).

The William Pecker Pottery

66) Red earthenware pot attributed to the William Pecker Pottery in South Amesbury (Merrimacport), Mass. (courtesy Ron and Penny Dionne Collection).

The William Pecker Pottery

67) Red earthenware pot attributed to the William Pecker Pottery in South Amesbury (Merrimacport), Mass. (courtesy Roger Pheulpin).

The William Pecker Pottery

68) Red earthenware pitcher attributed to South Amesbury (Merrimacport), Mass. (courtesy National Museum of American History at the Smithsonian Institute).

The William Pecker Pottery

69) Red earthenware pot attributed to South Amesbury (Merrimacport), Mass. (courtesy Old Sturbridge Village).

The William Pecker Pottery

70) Red earthenware pot attributed to the William Pecker Pottery in South Amesbury (Merrimacport), Mass. (courtesy Old Sturbridge Village).

71) Red earthenware pitcher attributed to the William Pecker Pottery in South Amesbury (Merrimacport), Mass. (courtesy Old Sturbridge Village); ht. 8 ½".

The William Pecker Pottery

72) Red earthenware pot attributed to the William Pecker Pottery in South Amesbury (Merrimacport), Mass. (courtesy Sam Forsythe).

73) Red earthenware pot attributed to the William Pecker Pottery in South Amesbury (Merrimacport), Mass. (courtesy Crocker Farm Auctions of American Redware and Stoneware); ht. 7 ½".

The William Pecker Pottery

74) Red earthenware pot attributed to the William Pecker Pottery in South Amesbury (Merrimacport), Mass. (courtesy Crocker Farm Auctions of American Redware and Stoneware); ht. 8".

75) Red earthenware pot attributed to the William Pecker Pottery in South Amesbury (Merrimacport), Mass. (courtesy John McInnis Auctions); ht. 5 ¾"

The William Pecker Pottery

76) Red earthenware pot attributed to the William Pecker Pottery in South Amesbury (Merrimacport), Mass. (courtesy Lewis Scranton Collection); ht. 8 ½".

77) Red earthenware pot attributed to South Amesbury (Merrimacport), Mass. (courtesy Dr. Brian Mills).

78) Red earthenware pot attributed to the William Pecker Pottery in South Amesbury (Merrimacport), Mass. (courtesy Sam Herrup).

The William Pecker Pottery

79) Red earthenware handled bowl attributed to the William Pecker Pottery in South Amesbury (Merrimacport), Mass.; ht. 3 ¼".

80) Red earthenware bowl attributed to the William Pecker Pottery in South Amesbury (Merrimacport), Mass, similar black glazed bowls have been recovered in Portsmouth, N.H..; ht. 2 ¾".

81) Red earthenware flask possibly made at the William Pecker Pottery in South Amesbury (Merrimacport), Mass. (from the Hilary and Paulette Nolan Collection); ht. 5 ½".

82) Red earthenware jar possibly made at the William Pecker Pottery in South Amesbury (Merrimacport), Mass.; ht. 8".

The William Pecker Pottery

83) Red earthenware flowerpot attributed to the William Pecker Pottery in South Amesbury (Merrimacport), Mass. (courtesy Old Sturbridge Village).

84) (Middle) Red earthenware flowerpot attributed to the William Pecker Pottery in South Amesbury (Merrimacport), Mass. (courtesy Roger Pheulpin).

85) (Left) Red earthenware jar possibly made at the William Pecker Pottery in South Amesbury (Merrimacport), Mass. (courtesy Roger Pheulpin).

86) (Left) Red earthenware jar attributed to the William Pecker Pottery in South Amesbury (Merrimacport), Mass. (courtesy Dr. Brian Mills).

The William Pecker Pottery

87) Red earthenware pot possibly made at the William Pecker Pottery in South Amesbury (Merrimacport), Mass. (courtesy Lewis Scranton Collection); ht. 5".

88) Red earthenware warmer that shares characteristics of wares made in South Amesbury (Merrimacport), Mass. and southern New Hampshire; ht. 9".

89) Red earthenware chamberpot attributed to the William Pecker Pottery in South Amesbury (Merrimacport), Mass. (courtesy Old Sturbridge Village).

90) Red earthenware jar likely made in either Essex County, Mass. or New Hampshire, possibly from South Amesbury (Merrimacport), Mass.; ht. 11 ¼".

The William Pecker Pottery

\> Stoneware

91a) Two gallon stoneware jug made at the William Pecker Pottery in South Amesbury (Merrimacport), Mass., marked "Wm PECKER;" ht. 15 ½".

91b) View of the gallon capacity mark and the "Wm PECKER" stamp.

The William Pecker Pottery

91c) Additional views of the jug.

92a) Two gallon stoneware jar made at the William Pecker Pottery in South Amesbury (Merrimacport), Mass. decorated with a stamped bird on one side and a stamped fish on the other; ht. 13".

The William Pecker Pottery

92b) Additional views of the jar.

The William Pecker Pottery

93) One gallon stoneware jug made at the William Pecker Pottery in South Amesbury (Merrimacport), Mass., marked "Wm PECKER (courtesy Raymond Burke);" ht. 13".

The William Pecker Pottery

94) Stoneware jug made at the William Pecker Pottery in South Amesbury (Merrimacport), Mass., marked "Wm PECKER;" ht. 9".

The William Pecker Pottery

95) Two gallon stoneware jug made at the William Pecker Pottery in South Amesbury (Merrimacport), Mass., decorated with a stamped flower; ht. 15 ¾".

The William Pecker Pottery

96) Two gallon stoneware jug made at the William Pecker Pottery in South Amesbury (Merrimacport), Mass., marked "Wm PECKER" (courtesy Crocker Farm Auctions of American Redware and Stoneware).

The William Pecker Pottery

97) Three gallon stoneware jug made at the William Pecker Pottery in South Amesbury (Merrimacport), Mass., marked "Wm PECKER." Appears to be painted with a scene depicting the Treaty of 1677 or the Treaty Between Virginia and the Indians in 1677 or the Treaty of Middle Plantation (courtesy Gloria Mitchell).

98) Two gallon stoneware jug made at the William Pecker Pottery in South Amesbury (Merrimacport), Mass., marked "Wm PECKER" (courtesy Crocker Farm Auctions of American Redware and Stoneware).

99a) Monumental six-gallon stoneware jar made at the William Pecker Pottery in South Amesbury (Merrimacport), Mass., stamped on each side with a bird and flower, the center of each flower is also impressed with a George Washington seal, as well as a third on the side inscribed with the initials "S.H." (courtesy Crocker Farm Auctions of American Redware and Stoneware); ht. 16 ¼".

99b) Reverse side of the monumental jar (courtesy Crocker Farm Auctions of American Redware and Stoneware).

100) Two gallon stoneware jar made at the William Pecker Pottery in South Amesbury (Merrimacport), Mass., marked "Wm Pecker," and stamped with a flower and bird (courtesy Bill Chapman); ht. 12 ¼".

The William Pecker Pottery

101) The jars illustrated in pictures 99-100 (courtesy Bill Chapman).

The William Pecker Pottery

102) Two gallon stoneware jug made at the William Pecker Pottery in South Amesbury (Merrimacport), Mass., marked "Wm PECKER" (courtesy Steve and Lorraine German).

103-104) These unmarked pieces are also known to exist stamped with a very similar fish as the known stamp used at the William Pecker Pottery (jug courtesy Crocker Farm Auctions of American Redware and Stoneware; jar courtesy Steven Spangenberg).

The William Pecker Pottery

105-106) Unmarked stoneware jar very similar in form to jars manufactured in Charlestown, Mass. in the early nineteenth century, although this jar is impressed with the exact bird and flower stamps used at the William Pecker Pottery. It is impressed with each stamp twice (courtesy Paul DeCoste).

> Bibliography

Barka, Norma F. *Historic Sites Archaeology at Portland Point, New Brunswick, Canada, 1631—1850.* Cambridge, Mass.: Harvard University Press, 1965.

Edwards, Diana, Steven R. Pendery & Aileen Button Agnew. "Generations of Trash: Ceramics from the Hart-Shortridge House: 1760-1860, Portsmouth, New Hampshire." *American Ceramic Circle*, Volume IV 1988.

Essex County, Massachusetts Directory. 1884.

Ketchum Jr., William C. *Potters and Potteries of New York State, 1650-1900: Second Edition.* Syracuse, NY: Syracuse University Press, 1987.

Kille, John. "William Pecker Jar." *Ceramics in America*, 2004.

Lagerbom, Charles H. *Jonathan Lowder's Truckhouse: The History and Archaeology of a Colonial Trading Post on the Maine Frontier During the American Revolution.* University of Maine, 1991.

Merrill, Joseph. *History of Amesbury and Merrimac, Massachusetts.* Haverhill, Mass.: Press of F.T. Stiles, 1880.

Moran, Geoffrey P. *Archaeological Investigations at the Narbonne House: Salem Maritime National Historic Site.* U.S. National Park Service, 1982.

(Newburyport) Daily Herald. February 6, 1850.

(Newburyport) Daily Herald. February 20, 1850.

Newburyport Daily News. April 8, 1902.

Newburyport Daily News. April 15, 1908.

Newburyport Daily News. April 7, 1909.

Newburyport Daily News. March 22, 1911.

Newburyport Herald. March 30, 1821.

Newburyport Herald. April 5, 1821.

Newburyport Herald. April 13, 1821.

Newburyport Herald. December 18, 1821.

Newburyport Herald. January 16, 1822.

Newburyport Herald. January 19, 1822.

Newburyport Herald. January 26, 1822.

Newburyport Herald. October 7, 1828.

Newburyport Herald. October 28, 1828.

Newburyport Herald. January 9, 1829.

Newburyport Herald. January 16, 1829.

Newburyport Herald. February 6, 1850.

Newburyport Herald. December 27, 1853.

Newburyport Herald. December 27, 1853.

Newburyport Herald. February 3, 1854.

Newburyport Herald. February 21, 1854.

Newburyport Herald. March 17, 1854.

Newburyport Herald & Commercial Gazette. April 11, 1817.

Newburyport Herald & Commercial Gazette. April 15, 1817.

Newburyport Herald & Commercial Gazette. April 25, 1817.

Newburyport Herald & Commercial Gazette. April 29, 1817.

Newburyport Herald & Country Gazette. June 22, 1802.

Newburyport Herald & Country Gazette. June 29, 1802.

Newburyport Herald & Country Gazette. July 2, 1802.

Newburyport Herald & Country Gazette. July 13, 1802.

Newburyport Herald & Country Gazette. July 16, 1802.

Newburyport Herald & Country Gazette. July 20, 1802.

Palmatier, Sean & Justin W. Thomas. *Potters on the Merrimac: A Century of New England Ceramics.* Newburyport, Mass.: Custom House Maritime Museum, 2019.

Sears, John Henry. *The Physical Geography, Geology Mineralogy and Paleontology of Essex County, Massachusetts.* Salem, Mass.: The Essex Institute, 1905.

Thomas, Justin W. "A History of Pottery Production Along The Merrimack River." *Antiques & the Arts Weekly,* September 20, 2019.

____. "Buried in Merrimacport? William Pecker, his pots and his kiln." *New England Antiques Journal,* October 2013.

____. *The Dawn of Independence, the Death of An Industry: The Pottery of Charlestown, Massachusetts.* Beverly, Mass.: Historic Beverly, 2020.

____. "Digging Into the Peabody Potteries: Archaeology and red earthenware." *New England Antiques Journal,* November 2017.

____. *The Moses B. Paige Company: The Last of the Peabody Potteries.* Beverly, Mass.: Historic Beverly, 2020.

____. "Utilitarian Redware in Massachusetts: The Chase family pottery." *New England Antiques Journal,* October 2014.

____. "William Pecker a forgotten pottery from Merrimacport, Mass." *New England Antiques Journal,* August 2015.

Watkins, Lura Woodside. *Early New England Pottery.* Sturbridge, Mass.: Old Sturbridge Village, 1959.

____*Early New England Potters and Their Wares*. Cambridge, Mass.: Harvard University Press, 1950.

____. "The Bayleys: Essex County Potters, Part I: Chiefly Biographical." *The Magazine Antiques*, November 1938.

____. "The Bayleys: Essex County Potters, Part II: Their Products." *The Magazine Antiques*, January 1939.

ABOUT THE AUTHOR

Justin W. Thomas is a collector and researcher into the history of American utilitarian pottery production from the seventeenth through the twentieth century. He has authored a number of research articles for various regional and national publications, guest curated a major exhibit at the Custom House Maritime Museum in Newburyport, Mass. about the local eighteenth, nineteenth and early twentieth century potters, as well as helped author the exhibit catalog, *Potters on the Merrimac: A Century of New England* Ceramics, and authored the books, *The Beverly Pottery: The Wares of Charles A. Lawrence, The Moses B. Paige Company: The Last of the Peabody Potteries* and *The Dawn of Independence, the Death of an Industry: The Pottery of Charlestown, Massachusetts.*

About Historic Amesbury

Amesbury Treasures (Historic Amesbury) is a partnership of seventeen unique historic sites managed by eleven organizations. Together, they cover four centuries of Amesbury's rich history, and as individual sites offer a deeper look into specific eras and aspects. For more information contact us at amesburytreasures@tnsing.com.

About Historic Beverly

The mission of Historic Beverly is to share Beverly's history with everyone through our 3 houses, 5 centuries, and 1000s of stories: by collecting and preserving Beverly's history; inspiring the community to engage with history; and making history accessible to all. For more information on our collections, properties, programming or publications, please visit or contact us at 978.922.1186 or info@historicbeverly.net.

About the Merrimac Historical Commission

The Merrimac Historical Commission works to document, record and preserve Merrimac's Rich History. For more information contact us at 978.346.9071.

www.ingramcontent.com/pod-product-compliance
Lightning Source LLC
Chambersburg PA
CBHW071420160426
43195CB00013B/1752